EMBRACING
HAP

BY LIZ ADAMSON

THE ULTIMATE GUIDES
TO EMOTIONAL FREEDOM

Embracing Happiness

Published by Diviniti publishing Ltd.
6, Elm Walk, Aylesford, Kent.
Tel: 01622 792866

© Liz Adamson 2000

1st Edition.

Printed in Hong Kong

ISBN 1 901923 46 0

EMBRACING HAPPINESS

Happiness is the Holy Grail that virtually everyone is looking for, but very few manage to find for any length of time. The reason for this is that we have not been taught what real happiness is and how to get it. This understanding is central to our being able to experience life at an optimal level. Without it, we continue to stumble around trying in vain to find the things that will make us happy.

I will endeavour to unravel this great mystery and give practical ways and means of embracing happiness in our lives as a matter of course.

HAPPINESS IS A STATE OF BEING

The main mistake that most of us make in our pursuit of happiness, is looking for it outside of ourselves. Happiness is a state of **BEING** and consequently, we have to seek and find it within. The reason that this misperception has been created is that the times when we can look back and see that we were happy are usually in response to something that **HAPPENED**. This then makes us think that we need happenings in order to be happy. In reality, the situations that create this feeling are just the catalyst that puts us into the state of being that is happiness. Many people will cite their wedding day or the birth of a child as being the happiest day of their lives. There are some people who will get married or have a baby expecting them to create this happiness and the reality is often very different. The happiness is not created by the event but by the feelings that we bring to the event.

The most exciting thing is that we can be in a state of happiness **ALL** the time and for no other reason than that we exist. This is available to every single one of us and it is the ultimate goal to which we can aspire.

The journey to find the Holy Grail of happiness is not a physical outward one but an emotional inner one. Many of us are unwilling to go into our emotional and feeling aspect because there are so many negative emotions contained in the same area. Happiness is a feeling and it can only be experienced if we are prepared to feel it. It is not a cerebral quality. Part of our journey to happiness involves clearing out and releasing our negative feelings like hurt, anger, fear and guilt and instating happiness in their place. Most of the things that we associate with happiness will also bring to the surface most of our negative emotions in order that they be healed and released. These include relationships, parenthood and our lifework. We can bring happiness to these things rather than expecting them to give it to us.

When we can understand the true source of our happiness, we can save a great deal of time and energy looking for it in all the wrong places. It takes very little energy to access it within us.

THE SOURCE
OF HAPPINESS
LIES WITHIN,
NOT WITHOUT

HAPPINESS AND LOVE

Happiness is a by-product of love and these two qualities are almost interchangeable. It is impossible not to be happy when we are in a state of real love. Equally, if we are happy it is because we have accessed love within us.

For many of us the times when we have felt happiest is when we are "in love". We equate our happiness with the love of that person. This then creates a dynamic where we make the object of our desire responsible for our happiness. Happiness and love come as a package and we experience them, not because the other person has **CREATED** them but because we have been helped to find them within us.

In many ways there is a higher expectation put on us to find happiness than love. When the majority of people are asked what they want most in the world, they will reply that they want to be happy. There are very few people who manage to achieve this wonderful state in any sustained form. We may wait patiently for the people and things that may come into our lives in order to make us happy. We are brought up on fairy stories that all run on similar lines. The damsel in distress, who is persecuted, fearful and unhappy, gets rescued by Prince Charming who falls in love with her and they all live happily ever after. Even when the cynic inside us knows that this is not reality, we still hold onto the dream that this will happen and that it is ultimately the only way to live happily ever after. We might even relish our victimhood and persecution, thinking that it is part of the journey towards love and happiness. After all we cannot be rescued if we are not in need of it. The reality is that a victim will attract a tyrant and not a knight in shining armour. We may then look to someone else to rescue us from the tyrant, and so the cycle goes on.

Both love and happiness are totally in our own control. If we are waiting for love in order to be happy, then we may have a long wait or be disappointed with the result in the end.

THE SPECTRUM OF HAPPINESS

Happiness covers a large spectrum of feeling. Sadly very few people even get close to experiencing the upper end of this scale. What many people may term as happiness may only just touch onto the lower reaches of the spectrum.

The spectrum covers feelings from contentment and joy at one end to ecstasy and bliss at the other. It is true to say that it would be very difficult to sustain a state of ecstasy, nor would we want to. The feeling would be too intense and almost certainly get in the way of our functioning in everyday life. However, we can aspire to experiencing moments of ecstasy and bliss tempered with periods of joy and contentment.

As we become aware of the ways in which we can bring happiness into our lives, our natural state will go higher and higher up the spectrum. In effect, we simply raise our energy vibration to a higher level.

The negative of this spectrum is of course unhappiness, misery, hurt and sadness. For the majority of the population, this end of the scale will be much more familiar. We just have the odd foray into joy and fun and then revert back to the normal state. This becomes the norm for most of us, so we don't question it. We see all our friends and neighbours living out a similar reality, so we don't aspire to anything else. Sadly many people are not even aware of the degree of joy and happiness that is available. This whole scenario can change when enough people **SHOW** the others that there is another way and that happiness is in fact natural.

There is also a neutral state where we are neither happy nor unhappy. We will often fall into this category when we disconnect from our feelings. We will almost have a sense of relief from this because it means that we have escaped from the tyranny of our own negative feelings. However, the downside of this is that in order to remove ourselves from our pain and misery, we stop ourselves from experiencing our joy and happiness. Disconnection will not work for us long term, since the negative feelings will constantly try to surface and come to our attention. We then find that we may try and avoid situations and people that may bring up our feelings and we become very limited. The answer is to remove and release the feelings that stand in the way of our being in our natural state of happiness.

Happiness is an energy and it therefore follows the rules that apply to all energy. Energy vibrates. It forms peaks and troughs. It has a frequency and the higher this frequency is, the more intense will our feelings of happiness be. We also tend to follow a cycle or pattern with our happiness. It is important to become aware of what our particular patterns are, in order that we keep the aspects that work for us and release and remove those that don't.

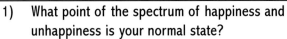

1) What point of the spectrum of happiness and unhappiness is your normal state?
2) Do you come into a neutral category?
3) Do you have peaks of happiness?
4) How often do these occur?
5) Do you have troughs of misery?
6) How often do these occur?
7) Do you maintain a neutral state without peaks and troughs?
8) Have you disconnected from your feelings in order to protect yourself from your negative states?
9) Do you acknowledge that you could raise the level of your happiness cycle to a point where you <u>only</u> experience the various aspects of joy and happiness?
10) Put together a diagram of your particular happiness pattern.

HAPPINESS AND CHILDHOOD

Most of our patterns with happiness are set in childhood. We are often unaware that we are simply playing out unconscious outdated patterns that bear no relation to how our lives are as adults.

When we are children, we are much more in touch with our natural state, which is to be loved and happy. We <u>learn</u> to be unhappy. If we look at children left to their own devices, they have a instinct for play and will find ways of playing, even in difficult circumstances. Children who are not allowed to express themselves naturally and are repressed, physically, mentally and emotionally, will soon lose this instinct. They experience high levels of anxiety, which will in effect block out any joy and happiness in their lives.

The first few years of life are key in forming what happens to us later in life. If we experience any difficult life changes at this time, it may seriously impair our ability to bring joy and happiness into our lives. Typical situations involve separation from one or both parents due to divorce, break-up, illness, death or abandonment. The resulting insecurity and fear make it hard to be happy. There are also many children who are abused from a very young age. An abused child is not a happy one and the absence of joy is often a good indication to others that all is not well.

Children are also very sensitive to the feelings and thoughts of their parents. If our parents experience very little joy and happiness and do not know how to create it, this pattern will be passed down to the children. There is a saying that is very valid and it is, "Families that play together, stay together." The families that fall apart and do not see each other as adults are usually very joyless and do not know how to have fun and good times.

For most of us our childhoods are a mixture of happiness and difficult or traumatic times. Consequently, there are two aspects to our inner child. I call these the joyful child and the damaged child. We will often alternate between relating to each of these, depending which one is triggered by circumstances. All of our emotions are created out of the child aspect of ourselves. The positive emotions are expressed through the joyful and the negative ones through the damaged one. The joyful child is very imaginative and creative, it is always thinking up new ways to have fun and enjoy itself. It sees life as one big adventure, which is there to be lived to the full. It is in touch with its spirit and it extends its joy and love to others without fear of rejection. The damaged child on the other hand, is filled with fear and anxiety, it feels powerless and may be very hurt and angry about the circumstances it has had to endure.

The degree of happiness we experience as an adult is often dependent on whether our joyful or damaged child is dominant. These patterns will be in our unconscious mind and will play themselves out, often without our even being aware of it or the cause.

The good news is that we are not stuck with this circumstance as long as we are prepared to become more conscious and to heal the damage that was done in childhood. All of this damage will have been created out of illusions. When we dispel the illusion and see the situation we experienced in a different light, we can begin to replace the negative feelings that were created at the time with joy, love and happiness.

We can also overcome our childhood patterning by becoming conscious and choosing how we think and feel in any situation, instead of reacting as we did before in similar circumstances.

1) Are you aware of the patterns of happiness that were created in childhood?

2) Were there any traumas or difficult times in the first few years of life?

3) Were your parents able to express any joy or happiness around you?

4) Did your family play together?

5) Did you have good times and fun activities that were laid on for you?

6) Were you left to create your own entertainment?

7) Were you a gregarious child that enjoyed mixing and playing with other people?

8) Did you laugh a great deal as a child?

9) Which child aspect is dominant in you, the damaged or joyful child?

10) If your damaged child is dominant, are you aware of the cause of that damage?

11) Is it fear, anxiety, anger, hurt or a mixture of all of these?

12) Look at how you perceived the situations that have caused the damage.

13) How could you choose to see them in a positive light?

14) Be conscious of your reactions to certain events. Begin to break the patterns of action and reaction by consciously choosing to think and feel differently. This is a gradual process and will need practice before it is perfected.

15) Bring happiness into these patterns.

HAPPINESS AND FEAR

I have already stated that happiness is our natural and normal state to **BE** in. We may think that if this is the case, then why do so few people experience it on a constant level. The main reason for this is fear. When we feel fear and its many by-products, we disconnect from our true selves, which is the source of our love and happiness. When this occurs, we become involved in an elaborate illusion that appears to become our reality.

Fear is always a response to something that has already happened. Having experienced it once, we fear it happening again. Even if it does not happen, the fear will often be worse than the reality of the occurrence. Indeed many people become relieved if the thing does in fact happen. When we are in a state of fear, it is nearly impossible to be happy.

When we are fearful, the thing we are fearing is not happening in this <u>moment</u>. We are projecting our thoughts into a time in the future where this thing may or may not happen. We therefore are not living in the moment. Happiness is a state of **BEING**. We can only **BE** in this single moment. This is a sure fire way of removing fear from our lives.

It is also necessary to recognise and understand that fear is the illusion that it is and not get caught up in the drama that is created by it. Instead, we can create a much more fulfilling scenario by choosing love, joy and happiness as the main components of our story. If we can choose the drama that we have in our lives, why would we choose fear over happiness?

1) Are you aware of how you entertain fear in your life?
2) Does it play a large part?
3) What are you afraid of?
4) How does this limit you?

5) Do you enjoy the drama created out of your fears?

6) Do you know the source of your fears?

7) Can you see them for the illusion that they are?

8) Do you end up manifesting your fears?

9) Is your prime focus of attention on what is about to happen, rather than what is happening?

10) When you become aware of this pattern, bring your focus back into the moment. Take a deep breath and acknowledge that in this second you are perfectly safe.

11) Know that you are responsible for how you respond and react to everything that happens in your life. By your response, you create your own reality.

HAPPINESS AND STRUGGLE

Struggle is a sign that we are not connecting with our true selves and our happiness. When we are in a state of struggle, we are going against the natural flow of our lives. Consequently, we are always tired and drained. All of our energy is channelled into just existing and surviving, and we never seem to get where we want to go without an almighty spurt of energy.

When we entertain struggle in our lives, there is often a built in belief system that if we were to stop struggling, then we would not survive. However, the reverse of this is in fact true. As soon as we stop struggling, our own natural flow will take over and lead us to where we are meant to be at exactly the right time for what we need and want and with a minimum of effort or wasted energy. We just relax and enjoy the journey with eager anticipation for what is to come. Everything is taken care of, a higher power within us is in control and we just need to make sure that we do not get in the way and interfere with the process. This is how life works at an optimum level.

When we give up struggle, happiness comes in as a natural part of the process. Each day, we wake up to all the possibilities that are available to us and yet we are happy to accept whatever that day brings, knowing that it will be perfect for what we need and want. With this understanding, we can enjoy every thing that occurs. We are set free because we are not dependent on any specific outcome.

Surrender is the key to letting go of struggle. All this means is that we give up the fight. Our ego will tell us that to surrender is to lose and we will then be in someone else's power and control. In this case the power and control goes to our own higher self where it will not be abused or misused.

1)   Is struggle a normal aspect of your life?
2)   What particular areas tend to be a struggle?

3) What would it be like if you didn't struggle?

4) In the areas where you feel this, are you sure that what you have created is right for you? The struggle may be there to show you that it is not working for you and needs to be let go.

5) If you believe that it is right, then you need to look at how you are approaching this area. Are you creating difficulties that don't need to be there? Is there an easy effortless way in which you could deal with this?

6) There is always a perfect solution to every problem. You just need to find it.

7) Can you change your perception of the situation to allow it to be positive for you?

8) When you find yourself in a state of struggle **STOP**. Surrender the situation to your higher self and relax and allow things to unfold in their perfect way.

I'LL BE HAPPY WHEN AND IF...

In our pursuit of happiness, most of us have a mental list of things that would **MAKE** us happy. Those of us that are the active doers in the world will then go after these things with the goal of happiness in mind. If we are naturally passive, we will also have a mental list but we will wait for these things to come to us. Unfortunately neither of these methods actually work. We often get more pleasure from the anticipation of the happiness we may have than anything that is actually manifested in this way.

When we project out our needs, wants and desires, we are actually saying that we lack these things and that is why we want them. The Universe is a wonderful mirror and it will reflect back to us what we have put out. We may <u>think</u> that if we are sending out a clear message for what we want then that is what we should get back. In reality, we are putting out a message of lack and lack is what returns to us. Even if we get the thing we think will make us happy, the element of joy and happiness will not live up to our expectations. Happiness is a state of being not having.

The "I'll Be Happy When..." syndrome is probably the thing that motivates most of us in what we do in our lives. This process always puts happiness in the future and only then if we get the things we want. However the future never comes, there is only now and if we are not happy now, we will not be happy in the future either.

Some common "I'll Be Happy When..." scenarios are as follows. "I'll be happy when I find my perfect job." "I'll be happy when I am in a loving relationship." "I'll be happy when I win the lottery or have lots of money." "I'll be happy when I look like Cindy Crawford." Some of these will be very tall orders to fill. Even if we get these things, they very rarely produce the desired effect. In fact in many cases they simply magnify our negative feelings.

We do not feel good enough or deserving or we fear losing the thing that we have got. Many people who have suddenly won a lot of money have found that far from bringing them happiness, it created a great deal of misery.

There is another syndrome that I call the "I'll be happy if…" This differs from the "I'll be happy when…" It involves a much nearer time frame and it usually gives two alternatives, one of which will create a sense of happiness and the other won't. The happiness provided will be short lived and once spent, we will need to look for our next "I'll be happy if…" situation. Examples of this might be. "I'll be happy if my team win on Saturday." "I'll be happy if the object of my desire rings me tonight." "I'll be happy if it doesn't rain when we have our picnic." We can see from these instances that this pattern renders us totally powerless. We have put our happiness in the control of forces or people that we have no power over. This can make us a victim and very passive.

Both of these syndromes make us dependent on outside forces for our happiness. There is nothing outside of ourselves that can **MAKE** us happy. There are certain situations that can act as a catalyst to our finding our happiness within. However, we do not **NEED** to have a catalyst in order to access it, we can simply choose to do so.

When we put conditions and terms onto our happiness, we will either create a win, lose situation or in the case of "I'll be happy when..." we may even set ourselves up for a lose, lose scenario. What we want is to create a sense that no matter what happens, we can still be happy. This is our ultimate goal in the joy stakes. In order to have this, we have to set it up. We could say "I'll be happy if my boyfriend asks me out tonight." We could also say "I'll be happy if he doesn't, because I will have a long hot bath and curl up with a good book." Both options create a win for ourselves.

When I look back at the things that I thought would make me happy in my teens and twenties, I can see with the benefit of hindsight that it would have been disastrous if I had got them. What I did in fact do, get and experience, I can see now were perfect for me and where I was meant to go, do and be. If I take this knowledge and project it into my future, I can see the futility of wanting any particular outcome. Instead, I can wait and see what presents itself, knowing that it will take me to where I am meant to go. I can enjoy this journey and be happy knowing that a higher power is working for me.

1) Do you have a mental list of things that would make you happy?
2) Write out this list in order of importance.
3) How many of these things are in your power to create?
4) What stops you from creating them?
5) Look at the other things on your list. Do you actively go out and seek them or do you wait for them to come to you?
6) Do you put conditions on your happiness?

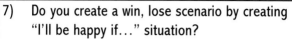

7) Do you create a win, lose scenario by creating "I'll be happy if…" situation?

8) Even when you win this lottery, how long does your happiness last for?

9) How do you react when you lose?

10) Can you acknowledge that your happiness is totally in your own control?

11) Look back at your life. Did you get the things that you thought would make you happy?

12) Did you feel good?

13) Can you see that some of the things you wanted would not have been right for you?

14) Did you waste energy trying to make these things happen?

15) Can you accept that whatever is right for your growth and evolution, will be presented to you. Whatever you choose to run with is up to you.

HAPPINESS AND RELATIONSHIPS

For most of us, our need to be in a relationship is in order to experience love and happiness. We are brought up on the belief that once we find the **ONE** person that will make us feel loved, we will live happily ever after. This particular myth has probably created more misery in the world than anything else.

In the early phases of a relationship, we connect with our own true loving selves and we do have a sense of happiness. At this point, we buy into the myth and we think we have met the <u>one</u> and nothing but happiness lies ahead for us. When we disconnect from our true selves as inevitably we do, we think this is because this person is in fact **NOT** the one. We then either extricate ourselves from the relationship and carry on with our search or we try to get back the feelings that we had at the beginning of the relationship.

When we are in a relationship, the child aspect of ourselves will often come to the forefront. If that child is predominantly the joyful child then we bring this level of joy, fun and play into the relationship and it will be considerably enriched as a result. However, if our damaged, wounded child is in the forefront, there will be very little happiness and possibly a great deal of misery and abuse. These relationships, which abound, bear very little similarity to the fairy story scenarios we have constantly been fed. For most of us, we alternate between our joyful and wounded child. It is important to note that people who are deeply damaged may not be capable of having a loving, happy, fulfilling relationship, without first healing these wounds.

Most relationships are based on needs and dependency. When we get our needs met by our partner, we feel loved and we have a sense of happiness. As the relationship progresses, we tend to get fewer and fewer of our needs met. Pressures, like children, jobs, money and the home will often take precedence over our meeting our partner's needs. When our needs are not met, we feel unloved and unhappy. We then blame our partner for this state of affairs and we will consciously ensure that we meet fewer of our partner's needs. This then creates a downward spiral, which ends the relationship with a great deal of acrimony and hurt. Our fear of being hurt again may prevent us from getting into other relationships.

The fact is that no one is able to meet all our needs all the time. We give our power away by expecting them to. We lay our happiness at the feet of our partner and we are dependent on them to give it to us. Once again, when we put our happiness onto an external situation, it will never work for us. Instead, we can see that we are the only ones who can access our joy, love and happiness. We then bring these qualities to the relationship, rather than expecting it to provide them for us. When we are around a person who is happy, it cannot help rubbing off on us. This means that no matter what is happening with our partner, he or she feels better for being around us.

There is an irony in that most of us look to a relationship to make us happy, in many cases we end up being hurt or unhappy. We then shut away the very part of ourselves that will give us access to our own happiness. We get into a vicious cycle, which prevents us from achieving the one thing we have set out to.

1) Do you look to a relationship to make you happy?
2) What are the needs you expect your partner to meet that will make you happy? For instance, being romantic, giving you attention, looking after you financially or emotionally.
3) Are you constantly getting these needs met?
4) How do you feel when you don't?
5) What needs of your partner do you meet?
6) Do you withdraw some of these if you are not getting what you want?
7) How much happiness do you **BRING** to the relationship?

8) How do you feel when your partner is happy?
9) Have you been hurt in the past?
10) Has this caused you to withdraw or shut down a part of yourself?
11) Are you able to be happy even when your partner is moody or unhappy?

WE BECOME

HAPPY

WHEN WE MAKE

OTHERS

HAPPY

HAPPINESS AND THE MATERIAL WORLD

Many of us believe that material things have the power to make us happy. If only we had a red sports car or a house in the country or the latest hi-fi equipment, we would be happy. We may even get obsessive about the object of our desire. All of our discontent is laid at the door of our inability to have this thing. If we get the thing we want, there is a short period of triumph, before we realise that this thing does not give us the happiness we anticipated. It becomes taken for granted, we might not even notice that we have it. We will then start to obsess about the next thing that will make us happy.

This pattern is often created in childhood. Children will often nag, cajole and manipulate until a parent gives in and buys them the thing that they want. Many companies make a fortune using this understanding. They tell children that their life would not be complete without this thing. They will then make a whole series of associated things. They may also make sure that the supply does not match the demand. Something that is unavailable is always more attractive. Children see other members of their peer group with something, then they will have to have it in order to be accepted. It is often this sense of acceptance that is unconsciously stronger than the need for the article.

Even when we know that getting the thing we want does not provide us with more than a few moments of satisfaction, it does not stop us from repeating this pattern again and again. Many women in particular will go shopping in order to cheer themselves up. We even call shopping retail therapy. However, while we may get a buzz in the shop from buying things, we often have a totally different reaction when we get home. Like any addiction, we come down from a high to a low. We may never use the things we buy and we often feel guilty about the amount of money we spent to get our fix.

When we look to things to make us happy, we are coming from a position of lack. We think that if a lack of something is making us unhappy, then if we get it we would be happy. This unfortunately is not the case. The sense of lack is caused by our separation from our true selves. The **ONLY** thing that will banish the lack is our making the connection. When we do this, happiness becomes our reality, no matter what we do or do not **HAVE**.

Money and wealth are hugely motivating forces in our world. Those that have it seem to have power, freedom, comfort, privilege and happiness. This can be very deceptive. Wealth often allows us to create an elaborate facade that convinces others that we have everything and therefore our lives are better than other people's. The reality is that there are as many unhappy rich people as there are poor. Many of the super rich are totally miserable. Their ivory towers do not protect them from their own pain, hurt and sadness. It is interesting to note that the word miser is well on the way to being miserable.

Abundance is created at the point where we detach from our need for the material and tap into our true energy. We get everything that we need and want but we do not put more emphasis on the outer material world than we do on our inner spiritual world.

1) Do you think that things will make you happy?
2) Is there anything that you have set your sights on at the moment?
3) Do you anticipate how you will feel if you get this thing?
4) Have you noticed in the past, how long your euphoria at getting the thing lasts?
5) When it has worn off, do you look to something else to take its place?
6) Do you tend to want things that are held in high esteem by your peer group?
7) Do you shop in order to cheer yourself up?
8) Do you think you would be happy if you were rich?
9) Do you envy the lives of people who are rich?
10) Do they seem to be happier than other people?
11) Do you put your main focus of attention on your outer material world?

INJECT JOY

AND HAPPINESS

INTO EVERY

WORD, THOUGHT

AND ACTION

HAPPINESS, DRUGS, SEX AND ALCOHOL

We have just seen how many people try to use things and the material in order to make them happy. We have also seen that this can be a form of addiction that is very destructive to the self. There are other external substances that we use in an effort to block our pain and instate a sense of happiness.

The main ones of these are drugs, sex, alcohol and cigarettes. All of these can have a social and recreational aspect to them. We may use them to **FEEL** good. In the short term they may seem to work. The chemicals contained in them or released in us, will give us a boost and we will think we have found the secret to our happiness problem. However, because the feelings of happiness or contentment are not natural, we are going to need more and more of the external substance to maintain the feeling we got initially. Once we are hooked, the process of withdrawal is so painful that we would do anything to avoid it. The addiction at this point becomes just about surviving. We no longer get any good feeling from it, just a return to the status quo.

It is exceedingly dangerous and destructive to look for our happiness in any chemical or external substance. Not only does it not create the thing that we are wanting but it ends up manifesting the very things we were trying to escape from.

The reason that we look to these things to make us happy is that we are empty inside. Our emptiness is caused by our disconnection from our true selves. This leaves a huge illusion of space and emptiness inside. We then look for things to fill us up. Many of the things we choose will temporarily mimic the feelings of our true selves. They may make us feel loved, special, valued, admired, strong or powerful. The effect is always short lived because it is not coming from the source of these things. It is an illusion. When the effect wears off, we are once again bereft and empty. We then return to the only thing that appeared to give us some relief from the void. The cycle then repeats until we wake up to the fact that this is an illusion.

It is essential in the treatment of addictions that we learn how to reconnect with our inner selves and consequently remove the emptiness that has created the need for the substances.

1) Do you use alcohol, cigarettes, drugs or sex to give you feelings of relief or happiness?
2) Are you addicted to any of these?
3) Why do you feel you need them?
4) What temporary feelings do these substances provide?
5) Do you recognise that these are an illusion?
6) Can you realise that these addictions actually stand in the way of your reconnecting with your true self?
7) What would it take for you to give up your **NEED** for the substances?
8) Can you get support for doing this?

HAPPINESS AND FACADES

Many of us have created a facade of happiness that is not actually real. We put on a mask and present it to the world because we do not want them to see the degree of pain, sadness, fear and anger that we actually have. We stick on a smile and act in a jolly way and pretend to the world that all is well with us. We often end up not getting our needs met because we cannot let on to others that we need anything.

Most of us do not look past people's facades. We take them at face value and we believe the illusion that they are feeding us. We then mistakenly believe that everyone else is happy and content and it is only us that are a mess and haven't got our lives together. In my therapy practice, I have heard countless clients who were in abusive relationships or brought up in dysfunctional families, admit that to the outside world they seemed to be the perfect couple or family. We become very adept at putting on our mask every time we leave the house. We might even convince ourselves that this masquerade is true.

I find that I feel very uncomfortable when I encounter people who use a happiness facade that is very different from their real feelings. Many people in the limelight have this pattern. I think the discomfort is caused by getting mixed signals. Our five senses respond to their smiling face and friendly voice but our sixth sense is picking up very different signs. These will come from the hurt, fear and anger inside. This conflict means that we feel we cannot trust this person. They are trying to hoodwink us in some way and may have an ulterior motive.

In order not to need our happiness facades, it is important that we release and heal the inner feelings that obscure our TRUE sense of happiness. We know when someone is truly happy, they exude it from every pore. There is a radiance and glow about them that cannot be fabricated. It comes from their body, heart and soul. We cannot help being affected by those who have accessed their happiness, their energy mingles with our own.

1) Do you have a happiness mask that you put on for other people's benefit?
2) Do you think you manage to fool them?
3) How far removed from your true feelings is this facade. (The further removed it is the more people will feel uncomfortable with you. You may find that people seem not to like you even though you are being very nice to them.)
4) What damage or wounds need to be healed before you can dismantle your facade?
5) Do you pick up on people who are wearing a mask?
6) How do you feel when you notice this?
7) Compare this to how you feel when someone is exuding genuine happiness.

MAKING OTHERS HAPPY

Just as we may have the expectation that other people make us happy, we could also have the desire to make them happy. Sadly neither of these things are viable. Our happiness is in our own hands and we cannot put it onto others.

We may perceive that if we meet the needs of those around us then they will be happy. This will only work in the short term. Pretty soon they <u>expect</u> us to continue to meet their needs and they will revert back to their old patterns from childhood. We try to counteract this by doing more for them and will either burn out or become resentful of the amount of energy we are investing in that person with very little return.

The best way we have of helping others to be happy is to access the feeling within ourselves and to extend it into our environment and everyone that comes into it. Not only do they feel better for being with us but it also shows them that if they access it within themselves, they too can have happiness become their natural state.

The one thing that parents want for their children is that they are happy. They then feed the children a diet of their own fears, worries, hurts and insecurities. These are the very things that block us from experiencing happiness and love in our lives. Many parents also try to protect their children and in so doing expose them to the very things and situations they are trying to avoid.

1) Do you feel that part of your role in life is to make others happy?
2) How do you go about doing this?
3) Are you able to maintain this?
4) Do you feel guilty when you do not succeed?
5) Do you put your own needs aside in order to meet everyone else's?
6) How do people respond to you when you are truly happy?

7)   Do you feel responsible for your family's happiness?

8)   Are you made to feel powerless by the enormity of the task?

9)   Can you acknowledge that it is only by your **BEING** happy that you can help others to become so?

ACCEPTANCE
IS THE
KEY TO
HAPPINESS

PART II

BRINGING

IN

HAPPINESS

HAPPINESS IS A DECISION

In part one we have looked at what happiness is and what blocks it. In part two we will reveal the ways in which we can embrace it and make it a feature of our natural being.

The first thing that we need to make clear on our path to happiness is that in order to access this feeling there has to be a choice or decision made. It does not just happen to us, nor can anyone else make us happy or make that decision for us. Often when we have been happy in the past, we may not have been aware of actually making this choice or decision at the time. This is because the decision was made on an unconscious level. Our unconscious mind takes on board how we thought, felt and reacted to everything that happens to us. When we find ourselves in a similar situation, our unconscious mind dregs up how we felt and thought on previous occasions and brings those choices and reactions to the surface. If we are not consciously choosing to react differently, then we will repeat the patterns of the past. For instance, if as a child, we felt happy and contented when our mother read to us before bed, we may associate books with that pleasure and get a great deal of enjoyment from reading.

It is essential that we become more aware and make our choices on a conscious level. In every given moment, we are either choosing to align with love or fear. If we align with love, we will experience joy and happiness, no matter what is going on around us. Fear will result in our feeling hurt, frustrated, bitter, controlled, powerless or many other negative experiences. Our fear is fed us by our ego or lower selves. Our happiness and love are a natural part of our Divine, higher selves. If we make no choice at all, our ego will feed us our negative thoughts and feelings.

IT TAKES AN ACTIVE CONSCIOUS CHOICE TO ACCESS OUR TRUE DIVINE SELVES.

We may find that the vast majority of our time is spent being unconscious and passive. It is like the feeling we get when we are driving and miles go by without our even being aware of anything that has happened around us. We know we have driven competently, it is as if our unconscious self took over. We often become so deep in thought that we do not see what is going on. Our ego selves dwell within the mind. The way to access our Divine selves is through our feelings. We have to be conscious to do this and make this connection. It will take a choice or decision to do this. When we become unconscious again we sever this connection and will need to reconnect. When we are starting out on this journey, we may find that we disconnect very quickly and it may be a while before we become aware that we are unconscious again. Like anything, it improves with practice and understanding.

If we are not conscious, we cannot make a

decision about how we want to feel or what we want to perceive and believe. We are in effect robots who are programmed to think, feel and act as we have done before. Some of our programming will be positive, so we do not want to change this other than to enhance it. It may be necessary to remove our negative programming and to align it with how we choose to think and feel on a conscious level. If this is not done our conscious and unconscious will be in conflict.

1) Be aware that in order to have real sustained happiness you have to make a decision to connect with your true Divine self.

2) To do this, the focus needs to be removed from the ego mind and thinking aspect and put onto our feeling part which will connect with the Divine.

3) The simplest way to do this is to take a deep breath into the solar plexus and take your attention out of yourself. Look at and notice

your surroundings. Connect with nature, a tree, flower or plant. Keep breathing deeply.

4) Choose to see the perfection in this moment.

5) Allow the positive feelings to fill all of your being.

6) Note how much of your time is spent being unconscious. If you are conscious you are totally aware of everything that is going on around you as well as within.

7) Do you spend a great deal of time in your head?

8) Do you torture yourself with your negative thoughts?

9) Every time you become aware that you are unconscious, reconnect with your inner self and make the decision to feel love and happiness in this moment.

10) Happiness is a feeling and therefore it has to be experienced through our feeling, emotional selves.

HAPPINESS AND ACCEPTANCE

ACCEPTANCE IS THE KEY TO HAPPINESS.

If we do not bring acceptance into our lives, then happiness is always going to remain out of our reach. Acceptance means that we are happy no matter what is going on around us, no matter how others behave and no matter what our own short-comings are, we can decide to be happy. Acceptance creates unconditional happiness.

When we bring acceptance into our lives, we put our happiness in our own control. This is essential because if we are reliant on another person to create the conditions for **OUR** happiness then we may be let down. Acceptance creates a guaranteed win for us and also takes the pressure off other people to be as we would want them.

There are three aspects to acceptance, the first is self-acceptance. This needs to be mastered first since our outer world is a mirror of our inner one. Self-acceptance allows us to be happy with ourselves **JUST AS WE ARE**. It does not bring in any conditions that we have to live up to an idealised version of ourselves. Self-acceptance means that we are content with how we look, our talents and abilities and what we have created and achieved in our lives. This may seem to be a very tall order, since our egos will spend a great deal of time feeding us dissatisfaction with these aspects of ourselves. It is also important in our self-acceptance that we do not compare ourselves with others or think where we ought to be in our lives.

WHO WE ARE AND WHERE WE ARE AT
IS JUST PERFECT FOR US.

Built into this self-acceptance is the understanding that we are work in progress and are in the middle of evolving. Everything that is being presented to us is there to promote our growth and evolution, even if it is merely showing us how we do <u>not</u> want to be.

Acceptance of others is the next area of focus. This may seem quite difficult because the ego often projects our own dissatisfaction about ourselves onto others. We are merely judging and criticising a reflection of ourselves. Within acceptance of others our objective is to not need them to be any different than they are and not to condemn them for who they are. It is of course hardest to accept those who are closest to us and it is within these relationships that our work needs to be done. It is very easy to bring acceptance for those people who do not impinge on our lives. With people around us we may have to accept their annoying habits and choose to see them as endearing or amusing. We will find that when we bring in acceptance for the behaviour of others, we enable them to change and grow. I have often found that as soon as I have accepted an aspect of a person that I had a problem with, that aspect is no longer there.

The third area of acceptance is for everything that happens to us. It is really important that we do not pin our hopes on a specific outcome. If we accept that whatever happens to us is the best possible thing, then we create a win for ourselves every time. If we get the job we are going for, then it is right for us, if we don't then something better is on the way. With this area of acceptance we may need to take it one step further and not just accept the situation but look to find the good in it. It will always be there and as soon as we discover it, we raise the vibration of the whole experience. It becomes positive. Acceptance alone creates a neutral state that is neither bad nor good, it just is. The more positivity we can inject into our lives, the further up the spectrum of happiness we can go.

We have to be conscious and aware in order to bring in acceptance. If we are not, we will have reacted to a person or situation before we can choose to accept them. It helps to put out a message of acceptance at the start of each day. If we have a negative response to ourselves, other people or the situations of life, we will not **FEEL GOOD**. This then blocks out our joy and happiness.

Acceptance is one of the major lessons of life and we may be tested on it many times and in some very challenging ways. As soon as acceptance is rooted in our being, we will find that it will rarely be put to the test.

1) Can you acknowledge that acceptance can bring the freedom of joy and happiness, no matter what?
2) Are there things about yourself that you find hard to accept?
3) Make a list of these things.
4) These are probably the very challenges that you are here to grow and learn from.
5) Know that in this moment these things are perfect for you just as they are.
6) You may find that at the point where you totally accept these things, they may not need to be there anymore.
7) Whenever you catch yourself being negative

or judging or criticising yourself, **STOP**. Immediately say, **I LOVE AND ACCEPT MYSELF JUST AS I AM**.

8) Do you find it hard to accept people around you? Do you often feel angry, annoyed or irritated by them? Do you have long diatribes in your mind about the actions and inactions of others?

9) Do you take the moral high ground and see other people as being wrong or bad in what they are and do?

10) Apart from making you feel superior, does your criticism make you **FEEL GOOD**?

11) Can you see that each person is at their own level on the spiral of evolution? Wherever they are at is perfect for what they are here to learn and grow from.

12) What we think of others is more a reflection on us than it is on them.

13) Set yourself free by choosing to accept everyone just as they are.

14) Choose to laugh at or be charmed by their personality traits that might annoy you.

15) Start each day by affirming that you accept that everything that happens this day is for your highest good.

16) Relax and allow everything to unfold in its own time and place. Do not try and control events.

17) When confronted with a challenging situation, bring in acceptance and then look to see what the positive aspects of this challenge are. They will always be there and you will know when you have found them because you will feel happy about the situation.

18) It is never too late to bring in acceptance, even if you have already engaged with the negative aspects. **STOP** and change the polarity.

19) Acceptance takes practice but can become second nature if consciously employed often enough.

20) Acceptance will pave the way to experience **HAPPINESS** on a constant level.

HAPPINESS AND POWER

Happiness is totally within our own power. Yet for most of us, in our pursuit of happiness, we give this power away to other people and situations. This creates a dodgy dynamic which can render us powerless.

Power is a very emotive word. Many of us are afraid of our own power and consequently will suppress it or give it away. One of the reasons for this is that we may have a negative understanding of what power is. There are two types of power. Ego power, which seeks to control and disempower others and true power, which will only use its amazing potential to help others and to work for the greatest good of the whole. Unfortunately most of the examples of power we are aware of involve ego power. The power we are referring to here is true power.

When we see that the source of our happiness is in external things and people, we give our power away to these and we become helpless and power-less. Not only do we give them the power to make us happy but we also give them the ability to make us unhappy. We become a victim and will often attract a tyrant that does make us feel miserable.

As soon as we can acknowledge that the source of our happiness is in fact within us, we set ourselves free to be happy no matter what is going on in our outer world. It is in our own control and no one can take that away from us. When we are in this state, we also extend our happiness to include others, we may help them to find the source of happiness within them. This can then start off a domino effect whereby happiness can be the overriding feeling experienced all over the planet.

It is important to remember that no one can take our power, we can only give it away. Admittedly, we do this unconsciously most of the time. When we become aware that we have given our power away, it is simple enough just to take it back. This is done by choosing to see the situation differently. When we put our power in our own hands, we become **INVINCIBLE**. Nothing can touch us or hurt us and we are not afraid of anything. There is nothing anyone can take from us that it is not in our power to replace. On a conscious level, we may need to accept that the true source of our power is our higher Divine selves. This part, if allowed, is masterminding the perfection of our lives in a way that we could not even begin to imagine. We therefore surrender the control of our lives to our higher selves, knowing that this power could never be misused.

1) Do you put your happiness in the control of external people or situations?

2) Who or what are they?

3) Do you also allow them to make you miserable?

4) Can you acknowledge that the true source of happiness is internal?

5) Remove the power from each thing that you have invested it in.

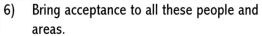

6) Bring acceptance to all these people and areas.

7) Know that in any given moment you can **CHOOSE** to be happy, no matter what is going on in your external world.

8) Acknowledge how powerful this makes you feel.

9) Notice that in this state, there is no fear, hurt or anger, nor any need to control others.

10) Know that no one can take power from you unless you choose to give it.

11) Recognise when people are in touch with their ego or true power.

12) Do not give power to those working with ego power.

13) Use your true power to empower others and spread a little happiness around wherever you go.

HAPPINESS, FUN, CREATIVITY AND PLAY

The most wonderful way to express happiness is through creativity and play. We may associate these qualities with childhood and indeed we need to bring this child aspect of ourselves to the forefront.

When we become adults, life is often about struggle and survival, we lose touch with the part of ourselves that knows how to have a good time. Fun needs to be an element that can be brought into every aspect of our lives. This does not make us frivolous or shallow, quite the reverse.

LIFE IS TOO PRECIOUS TO BE TAKEN SERIOUSLY.

Our work is meant to be fun, our relationships are supposed to be fun, our friendships, hobbies, leisure activities are enhanced by fun and laughter. If it's not fun, perhaps we need to ask ourselves why we are doing it. Fun is something that we can bring into everything we do, not something we expect to get out of it. We want to be around people who are fun, they will lighten even the most mundane of tasks or situations. A sense of fun is built into the state of happiness.

Creativity is an important aspect of happiness. It is the area that we can channel this energy into and it then can be made manifest in a more tangible form. This is how we can extend our happiness to others in a form that they can assimilate. We give pleasure to others through the joy and happiness we inject into the objects of our creativity. This can be things like singing, dancing, gardening, painting, cooking, decorating, story telling and many more ways. We can express creativity in many mundane ways like how we lay a table or arrange a jar of wild flowers or what we choose to wear. The possibilities are endless. Many of us have not even begun to tap into our many gifts and talents. Some we dismiss out of hand as being insignificant. Others we fail to develop because we expect to be adept without putting in the groundwork and practice that are needed. We often learn through our mistakes and we can only get better at anything we put our energy into.

An aspect of play that is needed is imagination. If we are in touch with our imagination, we remove limitation from our lives. The fact is that we can create anything that we can imagine. The more developed our imagination is, the greater the scope of our creativity. We ourselves and our lives are a result of our own creativity, how much more could we be if we use this facility to the highest degree?

1)   Is fun a natural part of your life?
2)   If not, do you tend to take things too seriously and look for the negative in situations?
3)   Do you see fun as being childish and beneath your dignity?
4)   Begin to choose to bring an element of fun into **EVERY** aspect of your life.
5)   What creative pastimes do you enjoy?

6) How often do you indulge in these things?

7) Do you allow more mundane things to take precedence?

8) Do you have untapped gifts and talents?

9) Are there things you would like to do but think you are not good enough?

10) Begin to do these knowing that you can only improve.

11) Bring creativity into every task that you do.

12) Do you exercise your imagination? It is like a muscle and needs regular work outs.

13) Can you acknowledge that you can create anything that you can imagine?

14) Know that we feel happy when we are completely involved in fun, play and creativity.

HAPPINESS AND EXPECTATIONS

There are many expectations that are built into our happiness. There are certain life conditions that we would expect to make us happy. These include things like the big relationship, an important job, the birth of a child, an exotic holiday or winning some money. However,

EXPECTATIONS ARE THE KEY TO DISAPPOINTMENT.

When we set our sights on a specific outcome or we expect something to make us happy, we usually find that it does not live up to its advance publicity. Often the outcome may offer something even better than we expected but we fail to see this because we are so set on what we wanted. This can be like trying to make a square peg fit into a round hole, when what we needed was in fact what we got.

When we have expectations, we are living in the future. We have already seen in our minds' eye what we want to happen. We have also gauged our feelings and reactions to it. When it does not unfold just as we envisaged, we feel disappointed and upset.

Instead of expectations we need to instate a sense of wonderful expectancy. Here we anticipate that whatever happens is going to be joyful and happy and provide us with whatever it is we need. However, we won't know what we need until it turns up. In this scenario we have already made the decision to be happy, we have also brought in acceptance for whatever happens, combined with the knowledge that this is the best possible thing for us at that time. This is a fail safe winning combination.

1) Do you have expectations about people, situations and events in your life?
2) How often does the reality live up to these expectations?

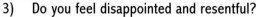

3) Do you feel disappointed and resentful?
4) Do you look for the positive in these situations?
5) Bring in expectancy instead of expectations.
6) Do not invest in any particular outcomes.
7) Decide to be happy whatever turns up.
8) Acknowledge how the things that you get are exactly what you need and want.

CHOOSE
HAPPINESS
IN EVERY
MOMENT

HAPPINESS IS IN THE MOMENT

Happiness is a state of being and we can only experience it if we are fully present in this moment. This may sound like an easy thing to achieve, after all we are all living in the moment. However, the reality is rather different. If we are in our heads and deep in thought, we will probably have missed the moment. If we are worrying or in a state of fear, we are projecting ourselves into the future. If we are going over a conversation or row we had yesterday or last week, we are not in the moment.

When we are in the present, our total focus of attention is on what is going on **NOW**. We are conscious and aware and we are able to choose our response to any external stimuli. Nothing gets past our eagle gaze. We are totally connected to our true selves and we can take full advantage of any opportunities that present themselves because we are able to recognise them.

One of the quickest ways of being in the moment is by putting the focus of attention outside of ourselves. If we consciously acknowledge something that will only be as it is in this moment. This brings us back to the present. We also need to activate all our senses including our sixth sense in order to get the most out of this moment. We only use a small amount of our sensory power and like anything else, if we don't use it we lose it. We rarely use our sense of smell for instance. Only very strong smells impinge on us. In order to use our sense of smell, we have to sniff and consciously take on the scents around us. Animals can tell a great deal by smell alone. They know how people feel, whether they are frightened or not and they can locate things by smell alone. We also do not use our sense of touch very much. Babies will want to touch and feel everything in order to discover it. It has been found that people who regularly stroke animals are greatly benefited. They are calmer, less prone to illness and generally happier people. Children will often hold or stroke the satin surface of a blanket for comfort.

The more we engage our senses, the greater the intensity of the experience we have in each moment. Our feelings of joy and happiness can be expanded as a result. It is also important that we work with and develop our sixth sense. This is our intuition and it connects us with our true selves. This gives us the guidance and direction that we need in order to live our lives at the highest possible level. It helps us to see an issue or situation from a loving perspective rather than a fearful one.

1) Do you live **FULLY** in the present moment?
2) Do you spend a great deal of time in your head?
3) Do you find that time goes by without you having been aware of anything?
4) Do people have to say things more than once in order to get your attention?
5) Do you spend time anticipating or worrying about things that lie ahead?
6) Do you relive or go over conversations or events in your mind?

7) Are you very observant? Do you notice what people are wearing or how they are feeling?

8) Do you listen to what people say? Can you pick up nuances in their tone that give away their true feelings?

9) When you listen to music, do you hear the words or notes?

10) When you eat do you stop and taste the flavours and textures?

11) Do you make an effort to use your sense of smell other than when strong flavours assail you?

12) Do you feel and touch things and enjoy the experience?

13) How developed is your sixth sense? Can you pick up impressions that are not provided by the other senses?

14) Work with the sixth sense by tuning into energy vibrations that are at a higher frequency than those detectable by the five senses.

15) Be in the moment by using all six senses and experiencing every second fully. Love, joy and happiness are the result.

BREATHING

Breath is one of the most important things we have, not just because it provides us with life. It is the vehicle that gets us in touch with the positive aspects of ourselves, it is also the means by which we can release and expel the negative aspects.

Most of us do not breathe properly, we use the upper part of our lungs and we take very shallow breaths. In order to make use of the benefits that our breath makes available, we need to take deep, slow breaths right down into our bodies. This can then access our feelings. If the feelings are negative, we can remove them with the breath. If the feelings are positive, we can expand them with it.

Our breath also connects us with our intuition and our true selves. It puts us in the moment and feeds the mind, body and soul. There is nothing more beneficial that we can do than learn to breathe properly and to bring it into absolutely every part of our lives.

1) Be aware of how you breathe.
2) If you take a deep breath, do your shoulders and upper chest move?
3) Take some time each day and lie or sit down. Put your hand on your stomach. Breathe so that your hand moves but your upper chest remains still.
4) Do not force the breath, keep it gentle and slow. Find your whole body relaxing.
5) Connect with your feelings in your solar plexus.
6) Breathe out any negative feelings you tap into.
7) Allow yourself to feel good.
8) Whenever you access positive feelings, use the breath to expand it.

GRATITUDE

Gratitude is a very important aspect of happiness. When we feel grateful for everything in our lives, we are putting our positive energy into everything we encounter. This will then expand the positivity that we experience and consequently the happiness. This even applies to things that may seem challenging or are providing us with valuable lessons or understanding.

Within gratitude we thank the people or situations that present themselves and we choose to see the benefits that are contained within them. As soon as we see the good in something, all the negative aspects just dissolve away and we are left with something that will make us feel good.

Gratitude needs to become a habit that we have. It can become an automatic response to everything around us. It may need to be worked on a little harder in situations that do not immediately show us the positive. For instance, we can look at a beautiful sunset or view and find it easy to be grateful for it. We may find this harder to do if we are in a traffic jam in the pouring rain when we are tired and hungry.

1) Do you use gratitude in your life?
2) Each day think or write down ten things you are grateful for.
3) Get in the habit of thanking in the moment of experience.
4) Challenge yourself by finding things to be grateful for in the most negative situations.

TIPS FOR EMBRACING HAPPINESS

HAPPINESS IS A DECISION – In every situation we can either choose to be happy or be passive and react as we have acted before.

ACCEPTANCE IS THE KEY TO HAPPINESS – It is only when we accept ourselves, others and situations just as they are that we can be truly happy.

HAPPINESS AND POWER – Our happiness is totally within our own power. When we give others the power to make us happy, we render ourselves powerless.

HAPPINESS AND PLAY – We can bring the joyful child aspect of ourselves to the forefront. Fun and play can be brought into every part of our lives.

HAPPINESS AND LAUGHTER – When we laugh it is impossible not to be happy. We can choose to see the funny side of every thing.

EXPECTATIONS AND EXPECTANCY – Expectations will lead to disappointment, live in a state of joyful expectancy for whatever turns up.

BEING IN THE MOMENT – Bring your focus of attention into this present moment. Use all your senses to get the greatest benefit from each moment.

BREATHE – Use the breath to connect with your feelings and to expand your happiness and release any negative feelings.

GRATITUDE – Express gratitude for everything that happens in your life. Find and be thankful for the good aspects of everything you experience.

I wish that you may embrace happiness in your life

Liz Adamson is available for one to one sessions, talks and workshops.
Contact: Flat 3, Hamptons, Hadlow, Tonbridge, Kent, TN11 9SR.
E-mail. liz@edenbook.co.uk

Available by Liz Adamson.

The Ultimate Guides To Emotions.
Releasing Anger	£4.95
Releasing Hurt and Sadness	£4.95
Embracing Love	£4.95
Embracing Happiness	£4.95

The Ultimate Guide to Relationships
£7.95

The Ultimate Guide to Abundance and Prosperity
£7.95

Contact: Diviniti Publishing Ltd.

Diviniti Publishing Ltd
PO BOX 313,
West Malling,
ME19 5WE
Tel: 01732 220 373
www.hypnosisaudio.com

...ford, Kent ME20 7LS
...6.
...viniti.co.uk